The ELL Special Education Evaluation Workbook

Companion and Training Document for the ELL Critical Data Process

Steve Gill and Ushani Nanayakkara

Introduction

This workbook is meant to be used in conjunction with trainings provided by Steve Gill on the ELL Critical Data Process. The report within this workbook provides the reader examples of some of the critical factors that we need to know and process. This is in order to determine whether a presenting problem is about language acquisition or is about disability, and how these factors can be considered and documented.

This example is not written to be a "perfect" example of the work in this area. The goal is to show the readers what is considered to be a strong example of a report in this domain, written by someone who has a real caseload. This example was created at a time in which Steve had 11 open evaluations for a 2 day per week school. This also provides the reader an opportunity to see examples and then process how they would have written the evidence. The reviewers who provided feedback during the editing process brought up some great questions. A few of those questions were not addressed during the editing so that there is an opportunity during the training to ask those in attendance the following:

- How would you write something that would make this clearer?
- Is the evidence already in the report and does it just need to be repeated "here?"
- Is there evidence that is missing?
- Would you make different wording choices to deal with some of the realities we face in the schools?

One reader was bothered by the repetition of some content. However, Steve has learned that repeating some content and helping to make the connection to that section of the report saves time and effort in the long run.

Steve created this example after having done case studies with numerous districts and agencies. Those examples came from asking districts and agencies to find reports to use as case studies during the second or third day of training. The instructions to the district were and are very simple:

- Find 3-5 students who are ELL qualified and Special Education qualified under the category of Specific Learning Disability,
- Make sure that the report is the first time they were qualified under SLD (initial evaluation or re-eval from DD),
- Take the first ones you find, don't go "hunting",
- Redact them and send them to me (Steve).

After reading somewhere between 150 and 200 examples, the pattern was clear. Within this set of reports, the vast majority had zero evidence of carefully considering and documenting a variety of sources (that line should sound familiar, given it is straight out of the federal special education laws (CFR)). Some reports didn't even document that the student was a language learner. Often the writer simply stated, "Language learning is not a factor." Within that second group, there was often no reasoning and no evidence. Finally, there were a handful of reports that had reasoning, but each of them was based upon something that was not actually true or accurate.

For example, the term "advanced language learner" is used on some of the state language acquisition tests. This term is usually referring to a student who is roughly half-way from being a student new to English to being a student who has passed the language acquisition test and is no longer qualified for services. When this term is referred to in the reports, the writer of the report will state something like the following: Given that Johnny is now an advanced English learner, Johnny's English is developed to a point that language acquisition is no longer a factor. However, this totally ignores the data regarding how language learners perform on state and national testing who have already passed through all of the language acquisition levels. The research often states that the students who were once considered language learners perform at the 32nd to 38th percentile when compared to their non-language learner peers. Therefore, there is no validity to stating: Given that Johnny is now an advanced English learner, Johnny's English is developed to a point that language acquisition is no longer a factor. This is part of the reason that each team that is evaluating a language learner for the possibility of special education eligibility needs to have a member who is an expert in language acquisition.

The style for writing this report is not like the style we were taught in college and graduate school. There are many reasons for this, but the most important reason is making the report "readable" by people who don't read and write these every day. Therefore, the usage of jargon should be highly limited. Steve has had the opportunity to have over 100 parents read and respond to redacted reports taken at random from within a large school district. The parents were very clear regarding less jargon and had a complete lack of interest in the characteristics of the tests that we use. The parents didn't want to hear scores, they wanted a description of how their child performed. The parents want to hear about their children as much as is feasible within the report. Also, Steve has been provided the opportunity throughout his career, across four districts, to complete the most contentious cases. He has evaluated judges' children, a senator's child, superintendents' children, special education directors' children, and even one student whose parents had taken the district to the supreme court regarding their other child. To this date, there has not been a single challenge put forth against one of his evaluations, even though he has completed these most challenging cases. This is only mentioned in the hope that those who see reports needing to be more technical will keep an open mind. Maybe there is something to this style that focuses on readability.

As you read this report and compare it to the information needed for the ELL Critical Data Process, think about the following:

1) What evidence was presented to differentiate language acquisition struggles from language acquisition struggles with a disability?
2) What would you have done differently? How would you have done that? What information do you still want?
3) What can you learn from this and take directly into your work?

The margins in this document have been enlarged to make it easier for note taking and writing of questions during the training sessions.

Final note: Steve has modified his report writing over the years to only include the data that is critical to the discussion that is occurring and to integrate that into the report where it aligns with the discussion. This was in response to feedback from the parent groups. Also, there are sentences

4

and paragraphs that are intentionally repeated with exact wording. The reason for this is to increase the likelihood that the reader can see the information converge toward the decision, instead of the reader having to remember what was written pages before. The recommendations within the report are with regards to areas of needed focus, not programs or approaches. This is a controversial topic, yet within the school setting it is rare that staff have the level of flexibility (due to caseload sizes) and/or the resources needed to take a large variety of approaches across their caseloads. Last, as noted on the following page, the IEPOnline format is used for this report. This format does not result in easy to read reports, but instead leads to districts having higher levels of compliance to requirements, also a controversial topic. This report is meant to provide an example of what someone can do while working a large caseload, using a restrictive program like IEPOnline, and working within a system that has many challenges. The challenges we face are not due to a lack of caring by educators!

EXAMPLE REPORT WITH ELL FACTORS

The name of this student is made up, as is the name for the school psychologist. The information is real information from a real student, though. Many small and random changes were made to the data. These changes were not made to change the outcome, but to add another layer of protection to make this information non-identifiable. The format is similar to the IEPOnline format, given that IEPOnline (or document sharing programs that are similar) are widely used across the country. Therefore, the flow of the report is awkward at times, as it is in reports created in IEPOnline. The document sharing programs exist to make data management easier and not to make for excellent psycho-educational reports. Also, no effort was made to make this a perfect example. The workloads that exist make perfection or near perfection an interesting goal. Instead, this is meant to provide a realistic goal with real examples.

Within IEPOnline, each core section (e.g., Academics, Cognitive, Observation) consists of three subsections, which are: Assessment Summary, Conclusions, and Significant Findings. The Assessment Summary can tell about what was done by the evaluator, the Conclusions can summarize what the evaluator found, and the Significant Findings can record the decisions of the team.

There is discussion embedded within the report regarding ELL issues and the determinant factor. The "Other" section of the report contains a summary of these issues. It is critical that you read this section carefully. I used this section in IEPOnline to bring the pieces of this evaluation together, given the pieces are spread across many pages.

There are notes to the reader, given many readers of this example do not have experience with IEPOnline. All of the following information that is not part of the report is in bold and italics.

Demographic Information

Note to readers: This section is not replicated from IEPOnline. In summary, the student was in the third grade, was the average age for a third-grade student, primarily speaks English at this time, but has grown up in a home in which Spanish is the spoken language and his parents do not speak English. The student will speak Spanish, but prefers English.

Reason for Referral

Note to readers: Please note that there is data included from a previous special education referral. Don't let that confuse you regarding dates and current versus past skills. Also, IEPOnline automatically loads that information into the document. For this example, some of that information was edited, but the majority was left as it was found.

Information from Previous Referral:

Academic difficulties

Information from Current Referral:

The skills gap between Esteban and his like peers, academically, has widened since kindergarten. The referral process has documented data regarding this gap and that data is contained within this report. Esteban's parents and teachers are concerned with regards to his academic difficulties.

Previous Strategies

Information from Previous Referral:

Small group

Modified Assignments

Title One Group

One-on-One Instruction

Imagine Learning

Work sent home

ELL services

Information from Current Referral:

Esteban has continued to be in reading intervention groups of the highest intensity available here at Somewhere Elementary, in addition to the other noted strategies.

Background Information

Information from Previous Referral:

- Spelling tests: 0/8
- Map Reading: 141 (standard 161)
- Title Reading Mastery tests: 4/5 and 5/5--but group has been moving very slowly. He was recently switched to a one-on-one group and also does Imagine Learning to support the ELL and reading.
- Fluency checks: 0/30, 1/30
- Map Math: 129 (standard 163)
- Mid-Module Assessment given in Dec: 0%
- Attempts all work
- Follows directions in class

- Can copy words on a worksheet
- Talks very little in class--will raise his hand but then not give a correct answer to the question.

Information from Current Referral:

Esteban is currently functioning at the 1st percentile when compared to his peers on school wide testing. Esteban's teacher reports that he is one of the two students with the most significant academic difficulties in her classroom. The other student is currently served with special education services. This is true for all academic areas.

Esteban is qualified as an English Language Learner. His parents stated that he prefers English and rarely interacts in Spanish, even though his parents know very little English. The school psychologist is bilingual and attempted many different interactions with Esteban in Spanish. Esteban made it clear through statements that he prefers English. Esteban was able to understand and respond to simple requests/commands and he demonstrated the ability to converse at a low level in Spanish (i.e., his vocabulary was limited to very common words that are likely to be used by his parents frequently in conversation). Esteban, in contrast, did not demonstrate any struggles when expressing himself in English. Therefore, all testing was completed in English.

Further current information is in the Records Scan section below.

Note to reader: Most evaluators are not bilingual or multilingual. Therefore, using someone to get an opinion of the student's skills within the first language can be useful. Use caution, noting some groups have strong opinions regarding special education and disabilities, and this can impact their feedback. Therefore, it is important to ask questions that have as little personal opinion as is possible, which can be difficult. When in doubt, determine whether or not their feedback leads to data that converges or diverges, then respond as needed.

Records Scan

Report cards from each year are showing "attempts the work with significant teacher support" grades in literacy and writing. Esteban achieved "approaches competence with teacher support" grades in language development and mathematics.

First trimester 1st grade report card showing "attempts the work with significant teacher support" grades in Reading Skills. Esteban achieved "approaches competence with teacher support" grades in describes people, places, things and events with relevant details, expressing ideas and feelings clearly and in learner goals.

Note to reader: There was not a second-grade report card in the file.

Esteban is a very positive, happy student. He is well liked by his peers and works well with others. He is very eager to learn, but lacks basic morphology and phonetic skills. Esteban is able to participate in classroom activities and group work despite his limited abilities and will ask for help when needed. Esteban is not able to read independently and struggles with partner reading. Esteban requests teacher assistance during assessments by asking for questions to be read to him.

8

Esteban has very limited writing ability and often cannot complete writing activities, even when sentence stems or prompts are provided. Esteban is able to participate in math, however, cannot complete word problems without assistance with reading the problem. Esteban routinely meets schoolwide expectations in the classroom, but does struggle at times with staying on task and not disrupting others' learning.

The school psychologist used the ELL Critical Data Process to evaluate Esteban's information. This is a very difficult case, given that Esteban has received limited interventions that were directly targeting language acquisition. However, Esteban has been losing ground academically when compared to like peers (e.g., other language learners within the school who also speak Spanish and started with Esteban in kindergarten here). Esteban's little sister is outperforming Esteban academically. The family has four children, and stated that Esteban is having more difficulty than the one sibling who was qualified for special education. Also, the family is very concerned regarding Esteban's lack of academic progress. The family stated that the older brother who was also progressing slowly has made significant progress in recent years.

Note to reader: In IEPOnline, as set up within many districts, everything that you have read so far would have been gathered during and for the referral process (determining whether or not to seek parental consent for a special education evaluation). The following sections contain information (the vast majority) that was gathered after gaining parental consent for an initial evaluation. The box around eligibility decision and recommendations to IEP team was added to emphasize the shift from referral content to evaluation content, given this is a training document.

Eligibility Decision

Note to reader: This section is placed where it would be within IEPOnline. This section represents the critical portion from IEPOnline. Also, the SLD Addendum is at the end of this document.

Meets Eligibility Criteria: Yes

Category of Eligibility: Specific Learning Disability

Summary of Qualification and Functioning: Esteban is eligible for special education services as a student with a specific learning disability. This determination was based upon using the discrepancy model. Esteban is performing well below the other students in his classroom academically, and well below other language learner peers with similar experience and exposure as Esteban. The report documents his functioning, qualification, and ELL specific issues.

Recommendations to the IEP Team

Note to reader: This section is placed where it would be within IEPOnline. This section represents the critical portion from IEPOnline.

Areas of Specially Designed Instruction followed by their description

Basic Reading: Esteban needs specially designed instruction in the area of basic reading. This instruction can begin with increasing his sight words and his phonics/phonemes skills.

Reading Comprehension: Esteban needs specially designed instruction in the area of reading comprehension. This instruction can begin with Esteban identifying key story elements and facts from text that is read to him (Esteban cannot currently read at the sentence level). When Esteban can read at the sentence level, he needs to begin identifying key elements independently (in addition to when read to him).

Basic Math Skills: Esteban needs specially designed instruction in the area of basic math skills. This instruction can begin with addition and subtraction of two digit numbers when carrying and borrowing are not needed.

Math Problem Solving Skills: Esteban needs specially designed instruction in the area of math problem solving skills. This instruction can start with teaching Esteban to identify the critical numbers and which word tells him whether to add or subtract.

Written Expression: Esteban needs specially designed instruction in the area of written expression. This instruction can begin with providing Esteban a bank of words that he currently knows how to independently spell correctly and working to make simple sentences from these words. This instruction can also include increasing Esteban's ability to successfully use the program Co-writer (or like programs).

Health

Esteban has historically passed his vision and hearing testing. Esteban's parents reported that he has not had any serious injuries, there have been no significant fevers, and there are no diagnosed medical conditions. The family reported that his birth was normal, the pregnancy was normal, and that Esteban met the developmental milestones at similar ages to his siblings.

Academic

Assessment Summary

Esteban was administered the Woodcock-Johnson IV (WJ-IV) tests of academic achievement. The WJ-IV is a commonly used test to measure reading, math and written language skills. The administration was completed by Jeff Smith, school psychologist.

Esteban is an English Language Learner, and there is a high likelihood that this fact is impacting his growth in the areas of reading, math and written language. Esteban was not tested in Spanish, in these areas, given that he has very limited abilities to perform in Spanish and prefers to use English whenever possible. At Somewhere Elementary, there are thirty students currently qualified as language learners and of these only two are qualified for special education services (those two were qualified prior to moving to Somewhere Elementary). The team at Somewhere

Elementary has not* been making referrals for special education evaluations to potentially qualify language learners for special education services. The team at Somewhere Elementary stated that Esteban was their student of most concern amongst current ELL qualified students. This supports that the struggles Esteban is demonstrating are notably different than other language learners and more severe in nature.

Note to reader: This is not necessarily a positive. The goal is to find the right students, students who have disabilities, whose disabilities are adversely impacting their access to their education, and who need special education. Language learners should have the same percentage as all students, yet sadly are about 50% more likely to be qualified for special education (within the roughly 2 million student sample Steve has worked on). Yet, the noted pattern for Somewhere Elementary does truly support how Esteban was different than his peers in this school.

On the MAP testing in reading and in math, Esteban has consistently scored at the 1st to 4th percentile in reading and in math. Somewhere Elementary uses the MAP and AIMSweb tests to progress monitor all students in reading and math for the MAP, and reading for the AIMSweb. Of the two comparison students, both of whom entered Somewhere Elementary at the same time as Esteban and had similar ELPA-21 scores, one of the students has progressed from very low percentile scores to scores in the 30-40 percentile range, and the other has reached into the 50-60 percentile range. The ELPA-21 is the state required testing for all students who are qualified for English Language Learner services and it measures students in listening, speaking, reading and writing. This test is given every year to all ELL service eligible students. This comparison shows Esteban making very slow progress compared to his like peers who reached the average range during the same period of time.

Conclusions

Esteban came to the testing sessions without hesitation and presented as eager to complete any and all work he was asked to complete. The classroom teacher and Esteban's parents have stated that he is always eager to learn and to work. Therefore, given that the testing is similar to classroom performance and Esteban presented as eager to work, the results are considered valid and reliable.

Reading

Esteban is a third-grade student who presents with late kindergarten to early first grade skills. Esteban's standard score in basic reading is 72 and his standard score in reading comprehension is 49. Standard scores have an average of 100 and the average range is from 85 to 115. In the area of basic reading, Esteban was able to correctly name many 3-4 letter words (e.g., man, them, must). Esteban tried to sound out many longer words, yet had very little success putting together the sounds when the words had complex blends or multiple syllable. That is, Esteban frequently had portions of more difficult words correct, but was unable to put the portions together to name the correct word. During the phonics/phonemes subtest, Esteban demonstrated similar patterns. That is, Esteban was able to get many of the sounds and blends correct, but he struggled greatly to combine the sounds to make words. The struggles were greater as the words became multiple syllable words. During the passage comprehension subtest, Esteban demonstrated the ability to pick out pictures from a group when given a word or words that represented one of the pictures.

Esteban demonstrated the ability to read single sentences when there was a clear picture clue. That is, Esteban worked very hard to compare the words to the picture until he was able to use the picture to figure out the words in the sentence. Esteban was unable to correctly read individual sentences as needed to complete the reading fluency task or the reading recall task. Esteban tended to not know or incorrectly substitute about 50% of the words within each sentence during these tasks (these tasks do not have picture cues).

Math

Esteban performed at the mid first grade level during the math testing. Esteban's standard score for basic math skills is 72 and his standard score for math reasoning is 77. Standard scores have an average of 100 and the average range is from 85 to 115. Esteban demonstrated the ability to complete single digit addition and subtraction by either counting, using his fingers or using dots. Using these same strategies, Esteban was very close to correct answers on items with a total above ten that did not require borrowing or carrying. Esteban did not demonstrate knowledge of borrowing or carrying. In the area of math fluency, Esteban completed a small number of problems when compared to peers. Esteban's methods lead to very slow work completion within math. During the math story problems (these are read to Esteban), he demonstrated the ability to add to or subtract from a small number of items shown in a picture. Esteban did not demonstrate a knowledge of coin values. Esteban was not successful when the math story problems required him to take information from the problem (that didn't have a picture) and use it based upon the information provided within the problem. Esteban did well on the portion of the testing that looks at patterns, until the patterns changed from those used in the examples. The school psychologist broke standardization attempting to understand how Esteban would react/respond (i.e., the school psychologist told Esteban that would not work and he had to try something different), yet Esteban continued to apply the same rule as earlier from the examples.

Written Expression

Esteban performed at late kindergarten level in this area. Esteban's standard score in written expression is a standard score of 54. Standard scores have an average of 100 and the average range is from 85 to 115. Esteban demonstrated the ability to correctly spell some 2-3 letter words (e.g., is, fun). Esteban's spelling errors after this point did not match either English or Spanish letter to sound patterns (e.g., "sal" for saw and "yotr" for water). Esteban demonstrated the ability to spell his own name, and he was able to create a four-word sentence "Thi boy is scade" to mean "The boy is skating."

Significant Findings

The team has determined that Esteban needs specially designed instruction in the core academic areas (basic reading, reading comprehension, basic math skills, math problem solving, and written expression). This determination is based upon Esteban meeting the numerical criteria for a specific learning disability in these areas, these delays adversely impacting Esteban's access to his education, and that he needs these services as specially designed instruction. The descriptions are listed in the section for recommendations to the IEP team.

General Education

Assessment Summary

The following section contains teacher feedback for the evaluation process.

Conclusions

***Note to Reader:** The following is copied and pasted from a teacher feedback form provided to the school psychologist. This form was created to balance the need for feedback with the demands of being a teacher. If there is something that isn't addressed in this form, it will be addressed during interview with the teacher as needed.*

The following is quoted from the general education teacher.

Which do you believe is most accurate, only pick one:

      Student is not a behavior problem __X___

      Student's behavior impacts learning _____

      Student's lack of academic skills impacts his/her behavior _____

Please rate the following on a scale of 1 to 10, ten being outstanding:

      Work Habits __6___

      Effort Level __7___

      Peer Interactions __8___

      Attitude Toward Work __8___

Esteban has a positive outlook and is always willing to give his best effort in class. He relies heavily on peer support and teacher support. He is unable to complete most assignments even with assistance. He is familiar with "Co-writer" and "Snap and Read" assistive technology programs, however, needs reminders on how to use them without explicit instruction each time. Esteban is a friendly student who has shown improvement this year, especially in regards to reading and comprehension. He is still significantly behind his peers, but when growth is evaluated, he has shown positive and impressive growth so far. Behaviorally, Esteban is an excellent student. He remains focused and on task most of the time and is easily redirected when needed. The work is very difficult for him in class, but he utilizes all resources to show his best effort.

Esteban is currently functioning at the 1st percentile when compared to his peers on school wide testing. Esteban's teacher reports that he is one of the two students with the most significant academic difficulties in her classroom. The other student is currently served with special education services. This is true for all academic areas.

Significant Findings

Esteban is a student who works hard within the classroom setting and gets along well with his peers and the adults. Esteban's core academic skills are delayed to the extent that he cannot

13

currently complete work independently within the general education classroom setting. Esteban remains engaged with the classroom learning by following along with peers and obtaining assistance from his teacher.

Cognitive

Assessment Summary

Esteban was evaluated using the Comprehensive Test of Nonverbal Intelligence - Second Edition (CTONI-2). The CTONI-2 is a test that is commonly used with students who are learning English and there is a need for a cognitive evaluation.

Conclusions

The CTONI-2 has six separate subtests that use pictures or geometric shapes across the areas of analogies, categories, and sequences. The subtests are scored such that the average scaled score is 10 and the average range is from 7-13. For Esteban, five of the six subtests fell within the average range, and the remaining subtest (Geometric Analogies) fell just above the average range. There were no subtests that indicated an area of weakness for Esteban.

Note to reader: As noted in the Introduction, during the interviews with parent groups who had read redacted evaluation reports, they made it clear that they are not interested in lengthy information about our tests.

During the testing, Esteban presented as very curious regarding the activities of the test. He was very focused on the items of the test, and presented as working very hard throughout the test (e.g., Esteban remained focused and trying items even when he had reached the ceiling of his ability on this test). Therefore, the test is considered to be a valid and reliable measure of his cognitive ability for the purposes of this educational evaluation.

Esteban's Pictorial Scale standard score is 111, his Geometric Scale standard score is 103 and his Full Scale score is a standard score of 108. Standard scores have an average of 100 and the average range is from 85 to 115.

Significant Findings

Esteban is a student whose cognitive assessment indicates ability within the average range. Therefore, the delayed abilities in reading, math and written language cannot be attributed to low general cognitive ability.

Social/Emotional

Assessment Summary

The Behavior Assessment System for Children, Third Edition (BASC-3) was completed by Esteban's classroom teacher. The BASC-3 is a behavior rating scale that provides information on a series of potential problem behaviors and on prosocial behaviors. The following section was completed by the current school psychologist, Jeff Smith, based upon these documents, interviews, and observations. Within the problem behavior areas higher scores are more problematic and within the prosocial areas lower scores are more problematic.

Conclusions

The scores from the BASC-3 fall into three ranges: within normal limits, an area of concern, and an area of significant concern.

For the classroom teacher, the following areas were within the area of concern range: attention problems, social skills, leadership, and study skills. Also, for the classroom teacher, the following areas were within the significant concern range: learning problems and functional communication.

The following is quoted from the teacher input form:

"Esteban has a positive outlook and is always willing to give his best effort in class. He relies heavily on peer support and teacher support. He is unable to complete most assignments even with assistance. He is familiar with "Cowriter" and "Snap and Read", however, needs reminders on how to use them without explicit instruction each time. Esteban is a friendly student who has shown improvement this year, especially in regard to reading and comprehension. He is still significantly behind his peers, but when growth is evaluated, he has shown positive and impressive growth so far. Behaviorally, Esteban is an excellent student. He remains focused and on task most of the time and is easily redirected when needed. The work is very difficult for him in class, but he utilizes all resources to show his best effort."

The areas of the BASC-3 that present with some level of concern appear directly related to Esteban's struggles with core academic skills. For example, the item rated as "never" within this section is the following: Offers to provide help to others. In Esteban's case, this is not a lack of a social skills, but instead related to the fact that he is attempting to complete the assigned work (with very low core academic skills) and he needs to rely on others for help. Also, it is very difficult to demonstrate strong leadership and study skills when he is struggling so significantly with core academic skills.

The areas of the BASC-3 that present as significant concerns are also logically related to his core academic skills deficits. The teacher rated learning problems as a significant concern, given Esteban is performing far below his peers in reading, math and written language skills. With regards to functional communication, Esteban demonstrated age appropriate communication skills when interacting in English (i.e., he was able to express all of his thoughts without a need to reword or rethink anything during the evaluation process). Also, when the school psychologist spoke to him in Spanish while walking down the hallway, he responded correctly. Another student stated to him, "You don't speak Spanish!" and Esteban kindly and clearly corrected the student in English and explained that he prefers English. The rated "highly" (indicative of problems) items in this section were explaining the rules of games and stating home address. There could be other reasons for difficulties with these two items that are not related to a lack of communication skills. In Esteban's case, parent and teacher interviews indicate that he presents as immature. This presentation was confirmed during testing and observation, and presents as linked to the low functional communication score. That is, he waits for others to do things for him and when asked a question he actually expresses himself well. During the waiting (the time in which he isn't asked specific questions), he tends to respond with incomplete sentences until directly addressed.

Significant Findings

The team concluded that Esteban does not demonstrate a need for specially designed instruction in the areas of social skills or emotional regulation. The scores noted above are either of relatively low concern or can be explained by the impact of his low academic skills on his classroom behaviors. Therefore, Esteban's behaviors are primarily a symptom of the academic difficulties and not a cause of the difficulties.

Observation

Assessment Summary

The following section discusses formal and informal observation of Esteban throughout the evaluation process.

Conclusions

Esteban was observed formally and informally throughout the observation process. Esteban presents as a student who is willing and eager to please the adults. For example, each time in which an adult worked with Esteban, Esteban worked hard to attempt whatever the task was for that time.

During the evaluation process, Esteban entered each session with a smile on his face and he presented with a positive attitude at all times. Esteban visited about football, given he was frequently wearing Seahawks gear it was an easy introduction topic. Esteban was easily directed during each task and stayed on-task without difficulty.

Within the classroom setting, Esteban was paying attention to the classroom teacher at the norm within the classroom or at a higher level. The evidence for this was that Esteban responded to teacher direction 100% of the time when the teacher provided a direction (e.g., "Group 3 get up to get your Chromebooks"). Esteban was observed during a task in which they had to use their Chromebooks to complete a spelling quiz. Esteban looked to the other students in order to attempt to mimic what they were doing. The school psychologist believes that Esteban was doing this because he could not read the words that were on the page. After several minutes of observation, the school psychologist interacted with Esteban and provided some simple instruction. Esteban followed the instructions and answered the following two questions correctly. Esteban clearly had seen this computer program before; however, the wording on the page is far beyond his current demonstrated skill level. Therefore, he had to click on virtually everything on the page, listen to the description, and then try to remember where each item was in the hope of matching the items later. If Esteban's reading level was at or near grade level, then only a small portion of the page would require the clicking and listening, greatly reducing the short-term memory load.

Significant Findings

Esteban has continued to demonstrate an eagerness to learn and participate within the classroom setting. There were some reports of distractibility, yet those are reported to occur most frequently when Esteban is faced with academic challenges that are far beyond his current skill level. Esteban demonstrates positive social skills and gets along well with his peers and adults within the school setting.

Other

Assessment Summary

The following section contains additional information that specifically addresses the fact that Esteban is an English Language Learner and that the difficulties he is demonstrating could be primarily related to this fact or could be primarily related to being a student with a disability.

Conclusions

The following information is meant to provide the reader context when trying to determine if language acquisition or disability is the determinant factor for Esteban's academic difficulties.

1) When Esteban is compared directly with two of his peers who speak the same language and entered kindergarten with similar ELPA-21 (language acquisition test) scores, Esteban has lost ground relative to his peers each year. That is, Esteban's test scores have actually decreased and their test scores have increased. Esteban, when compared to his same age peers on this test is not advancing. In contrast, one of his peers has made average growth and another has made exceptional growth within this environment. All three students speak Spanish, were born in the United States, and none of them have formal education in Spanish.

2) Esteban's younger sister is a student here at Somewhere Elementary. She is currently performing within the average range, and she is demonstrating skills similar to or stronger than Esteban's skills, even though she is two years younger.

3) Esteban is an English Language Learner and there is a high likelihood that this fact is impacting his growth in the areas of reading, math and written language. Esteban was not tested in Spanish, in these areas, given that he has very limited abilities to perform in Spanish and prefers to use English whenever possible. At Somewhere Elementary, there are thirty students currently qualified as language learners and of these only two are qualified for special education services (those two were qualified prior to moving to Somewhere Elementary). Therefore, the team at Somewhere Elementary does not test to qualify language learners for special education services and the team at Somewhere Elementary stated that Esteban was their student of most concern amongst current ELL qualified students. The school has achieved these results even though the ELL program is not clearly defined.

17

4) The ELL Critical Data Process was completed to better understand Esteban's history. There are no clear factors that have been noted within this process that indicated that more intervention is clearly needed prior to determining disability and there are no clear factors that are indicative of disability (e.g., a medical condition unknown to the team prior to starting). Esteban does have an older brother who struggled to progress and needed a great deal of additional help. The family has indicated that this brother is doing much better at this point in time.

5) On the MAP testing in reading and in math, Esteban has consistently scored at the 1st to 4th percentile in reading and in math. Of the two comparison students, both of whom entered Somewhere Elementary at the same time as Esteban and had similar ELPA-21 scores, one of the students has progressed from very low percentile scores to scores in the 35-45 percentile range, and the other has reached into the 55-65 percentile range. Each of these students has received similar intervention in reading over time, and the other two students in this direct comparison have responded positively to the interventions.

6) Esteban has demonstrated some language confusion when speaking with him in Spanish. However, Esteban has shown a strong preference towards English. Esteban's parents state that he rarely speaks in Spanish. During the evaluation process Esteban was willing to attempt to interact with the school psychologist in Spanish, but stated that he prefers to speak English. Therefore, the presence of language confusion does not help in determining disability, given his exposure and experience with Spanish.

7) Esteban's teachers and parents have been able to establish and reinforce high expectations for Esteban, and the interviews indicate Esteban works hard to meet these expectations (see teacher comments as an example). Esteban's parents also commented that he is a very hard worker and that he is eager to learn in school. Esteban has been engaged in the learning process each and every time the school psychologist has entered the room.

8) Esteban's PE teacher and Music teachers both gathered data over a 10-week period of time regarding how well Esteban appeared to be learning the lessons in their classrooms compared to four of Esteban's peers. Esteban's scores during this are within the average of the other students. Esteban's PE teacher and Music teacher both commented on his efforts in class in a very positive manner.

9) Esteban's father is literate in Spanish and he did read to him in Spanish as a younger child. Therefore, Esteban's had exposure to vocabulary in Spanish from his parents that is more extensive (i.e., individuals with literacy use a wider variety of vocabulary and more complex vocabulary). Esteban, as noted earlier in the report, uses English as his primary language. Therefore, Esteban has the exposure to this vocabulary, yet not the experience with the vocabulary, given he struggles to express himself in Spanish (e.g., Esteban can understand requests and simple conversation in Spanish, yet struggles when the vocabulary is more advanced relative to a student his age, and only expresses himself using very simple sentences and vocabulary in the present tense or present progressive tense). Esteban expressed himself without difficulties in English.

10) Esteban, during observation, remained engaged in the learning environment.

Significant Findings

Esteban is an English Language Learner, yet the team determined that his core academic delays cannot be explained solely based upon being a language learner. The evidence above documents that within Somewhere Elementary, the vast majority of language learners are successful academically. Also, Esteban's younger sister, with the same home environment, same language experience, and same school experience is doing well in school. Therefore, the team has determined that the determinant factor for Esteban's academic delays is a specific learning disability.

SLD Addendum

Note to reader: The following is modified from a section within IEPOnline that is used to document the model used for SLD qualification and to address specific legal considerations for this category. It is a representation of the section relative to important information for this example.

There is a portion that requires the input of the scores in order to meet the numerical criteria under Washington state law for SLD via the discrepancy model. Esteban met that numerical criteria (and well beyond that criteria).

Professional Judgment: Not applied in this case.

Basis for Determination: Severe Discrepancy Model

Educationally Relevant Medical Findings: There are no known or suspected medical issues.

Relevant Behavior: Esteban has been reported as having some struggles with focus and attention. The only reports of this coincide with when Esteban is presented work, during whole class activity, that he cannot independently understand or complete. Therefore, the behaviors are seen as a result of the academic delays and not a cause of the academic delays (especially when combined with other information noted within the body of the report).

Effects of Environment, cultural, or economic disadvantage as determined by the team: Esteban is an English Language Learner. This has been discussed throughout the report. The team determined that, although a factor in the severity of Esteban's delays, this is not the determinant factor for the delays. That is, the delays would exist even if Esteban was not an English Language Learner. Therefore, the determinant factor in the delays is a specific learning disability.

End of Report

Workbook Summary

The purpose of this workbook is to provide the reader an example of how factors that are critical to determining whether a struggling language learner is struggling due to the normal challenges faced by all language learners or if the student might also have a disability. The report wasn't created to be a "gold standard" in a world in which time is not a factor. Instead, the report is written in the IEPOnline format (which creates challenges regarding flow) and was written during a time in which my caseload was extremely difficult. Therefore, this is believed to be a good example of what everyone can achieve, even with the challenges we face in our day-to-day work. The most critical factors are:

- Making the report readable for parents and teachers (less jargon, less about tests, more about the student and how they are functioning),
- Making sure the parents and teachers know where the student is functioning in the areas of needed service (if they are qualifying),
- Making sure that the reader has evidence-based reasons as to why or why not there is a disability in addition to normal challenges found within our language learners.

Last, this was written to be used during the 2-4 day trainings that Steve provides on the ELL Critical Data Process. Therefore, a few of the things that can be critiqued (e.g., Why did you do ____? Or, Why didn't you do _____?) exist in this example in order to help create discussions during the trainings. There is a very specific line in the report just for this purpose. So, please do think about what you would have done differently. Take everything that you find useful from this and integrate it into your work, even if that involves something that you would do differently.

Acknowledgments

A special thank you to Mikael Olson, Tracy Pennington-Branen, Rebekah Hereth, Laurie Engelback, and Deb Wagner for their valuable and thoughtful insights during this project.

Steve Gill Biography

Steve's first job in education, before he became a school psychologist, was as a driver's education teacher. Then Steve had a wonderful opportunity to study school psychology and work at the university, so he followed that path.

Steve started his career as a school psychologist in a district with a large ELL population. There he realized how little he had learned about language learners prior to this experience. Over the years, he completed graduate work in ELL studies, eventually creating the ELL Critical Data Process. As of writing this, Steve has trained over 10,000 educators on the process across more than 300 school districts in multiple states.

Steve and Ushani (Steve's wife and co-author) have five books for sale on amazon.com. The first book, *The ELL Critical Data Process- Second Edition,* is a resource for learning professionals for determining whether more interventions are needed or if a special education referral is a reasonable option. Our second book, *Evaluating ELL Students for the Possibility of Special Education Qualification* focuses on the special education evaluation process for language learners and how to potentially achieve appropriate identification rates. Our third book, *Special Education Referral or Not*, is about using a matrix based approach with non-language learners. Our fourth book, *ELL Teachers and Special Education*, is a self-study or group study for ELL teachers to learn more about special education. Our fifth book, *Processing Perspective, Examining Beliefs, Biases and Reality Through Stories*, is a book that uses educator stories to help people see different perspectives and analyze the lens we each look through to view the world.

Steve is currently the President of the Washington State Association of School Psychologists.

Brief Overview of the 2-Day Training Program

Day 1

Section 1:

The first section of the training covers background issues, problems, laws, and research needed to assist staff in addressing the belief systems of others, and their own belief systems, that are impacting the progress in this field. The content focuses on understanding the relationship between acculturation, belief systems, practices and results.

Section 2:

The second section of the training addresses how children qualify for special education services with a focus on ELL specific issues that arise during qualification. This includes how to reduce the problems and core issues that lead to disproportionality, while breaking down the problem to three main areas of qualification.

Section 3:

The third section focuses on training those in attendance on how to complete the ELL Critical Data Process. This is the process created by Steve that helps staff to gather the most critical data, follow a structured process, and create a product that helps them to see whether more interventions are needed or if a special education referral is a reasonable option. The ELL Critical Data Process brings key staff members to the table and structures the discussions so that a student's needs are better understood.

Day 2 has three options:

Option 1:

The third section from above, focusing on the ELL Critical Data Process is repeated for a select group of people who will be leaders within their schools, districts, and/or agency. There will be about 1 hour of additional time. To increase the understanding of the process and implementation of the process, the groups will be asked to have discussions frequently and asked to share their thoughts and questions to measure understanding.

Then, the group will work through 2-3 cases studies. These will be real cases from their schools and/or agency, using evaluation documents that have been redacted. This will be done in part to help increase the understanding of correct implementation of the ELL Critical Data Process and in part to help emphasize how critical it is to have, process, and document data within the process of determining whether or not a language learner has a disability.

Option 2:

Preschool ELL CDP Training Day (approximately 4 ½ hours)

This option allows for a focus on preschool issues and is usually just attended by the preschool staff.

Section 1:

The first section of the training covers background issues, problems, laws, and research needed to assist staff in addressing the belief systems of others, and their own belief systems, that are impacting the progress in this field. The content focuses on understanding the relationship between acculturation, belief systems, practices and results.

Section 2:

The second section focuses on training those in attendance on how to complete the Preschool Version of the ELL Critical Data Process. This is the process created by Steve that helps staff to gather the most critical data, follow a structured process, and create a product that helps them to see whether more interventions are needed or if a special education referral is a reasonable option. The Preschool Version of the ELL Critical Data Process brings key staff members to the table and structures the discussions so that a student's needs are better understood. The Preschool Version focuses less on measured data (given there is far less available) and more on specific comparisons of the child's development in key areas as compared to like peers' development in the same areas, focusing on the LE^{3}AP process.

Option 3:

The day one training is spread across two days and has additional activities and case studies. The case study data is created by your district staff and the matrix is applied to that data (and additional data is added as needed by Steve). Additionally, the staff will (on day 1 and day 2) use a KWL learning process as part of their learning. The KWL process has the staff write about and monitor what they KNOW (K) regarding the topic, what they WONDER/WANT TO KNOW (W), and what they have LEARNED (L). The staff complete this in small groups to check for consistency and ask questions as needed.

Brief Overview of the 3 or 4 Day Training Program

This is accomplished through combining the different options for day two noted above. A common three-day training can include:

· the normal first day of training for all

· a second day that focuses on the Preschool ELL Critical Data Process

· a third day that is the first option for day two of the two day training described above, that repeats the K-12 ELL Critical Data Process (with additional time) and includes the case studies.

Additional Trainings:

Steve also provides each of the sections above as individual trainings at state conferences or for local districts, depending upon their requests.

Training is often customized by request.

Steve has training modules on the material from the books *Special Education Referral or Not*, *Processing Perspectives*, and also a facilitated training on the *ELL Teachers and Special Education*.

An example of an additional training that Steve offers is the 90-120 minute training based upon his and Ushani's sixth book, *Processing Perspectives:*

This training utilizes research, data and educators' stories to help us examine how our perspectives can have a direct impact on the students we are serving. The research and stories help us to look at the difference between perspective and reality. The stories were written by educators and chosen by Steve and Ushani to help provide another way in which to look at a problem or challenge that we face within our journey as educators. Creating an opportunity for new approaches to challenges via new perspectives.

Note to reader: It was important to us to make this available within Amazon.com and the minimum number of pages required us to add three pages, so we made the choice to add the training information. I can be reached through my website at stevegillell.com

Made in United States
North Haven, CT
22 May 2023

36861709R00015